Happy Christn
I hope you en
of 2020...with
Lord —   and know that there is,

NOTHING ORDINARY ABOUT YOU

INSPIRING AND MOTIVATIONAL WORDS FROM A CHRISTIAN PERSPECTIVE

from Elaine & Jeremy

X y x

See you In 2021!

VICTORIA & GIBSON IKORO

Published by Victoria Press LTD
ISBN: 978-1-9160085-1-9
www.victorspress.com
info@victorspress.com

Also by Victoria Ikoro
Lift Them Up: 31 Scripture-based promises to
pray over your children.

Note: unless otherwise stated, all scriptures were taken from the
New King James Version of the Bible.

Dedication

This book is dedicated to God Almighty.

Contents

Nothing Ordinary about You

*I said, "You are gods, and all of you are children
of the Most High.*

(Psalm 82:6)

A s Christians, we must constantly remind ourselves that
there is nothing ordinary about us. We can live a
supernatural life because the Spirit of the almighty God lives
inside of us. This is the same Spirit who raised Jesus from the
dead, parted the red sea, that gave sight to blind people.

What is ordinary about someone whom the Spirit of God
lives in, someone the creator of
the universe calls a friend? What is
ordinary about the one whom God
has given the power to trample on
serpents and scorpions and over all
the power of the enemy? I think the
devil is happy when as children of
God, we do not put to good use the
power that God has graciously given us.

> **Even though we may
> have challenges
> here on earth,
> we should not be
> overwhelmed with
> them that we forget
> who we carry on the
> inside of us.**

Even though we may have challenges here on earth, we should not be overwhelmed with them that we forget who we carry on the inside of us. God has made each and every one of us unique and when we cooperate with the Spirit of God we can do exploits for God. Let us exercise our faith and use the power and authority God has given us for good works. Intercede for your family, your spouse, your children, your community and your nation. As Christians, we have the power to command our day and circumstances around us to conform to God's will. We can act in faith, pray in the spirit, and cause great things to manifest in the physical.

> *You are gods, and all of you are children of the Most High.*
>
> (Psalm 82:6)

This is a "faith lifter" scripture for me. Anytime I remember that God says I am His child, and I am a god, I know any unpleasant circumstances around me must go. By faith, I can speak scriptures to counter negative situations and believe my Father in heaven to bring His will to pass.

Encourage Yourself

But David strengthened himself in the Lord his God.

(1 Samuel 30:6)

E NCOURAGEMENT IS A powerful tool needed for success. Many people either succeed or fail in their adventures depending on whether they were encouraged or not. Discouragement is the opposite of encouragement. When courage is gone, you are almost left with nothing to push through.

The challenge many people face is that they don't get the encouragement they need from others. The closest people to you might be the ones discouraging you. You may also be discouraged by situations, which you can't even control. The good news is "You can control yourself." You can decide to encourage yourself. That's

> **The good news is "You can control yourself." You can decide to encourage yourself. That's what David did. He encouraged himself in the Lord (1 Samuel 30:6).**

what David did. He encouraged himself in the Lord (1 Samuel 30:6).

It's a test when the closest and dearest people to you tell you to "Curse God and die." How would you respond if you were told that? I have a suggestion. Why not say:

- I know my Redeemer lives.
- I can do all things through Christ who strengthens me.
- I am more than a conqueror in Christ.
- My future is glorious
- God has great plans for me. Eyes have not seen. Ears have not heard what God has prepared for those who love Him.

Finally, brothers, whatever is true, whatever is noble, whatever is right, whatever is pure, whatever is lovely, whatever is admirable--if anything is excellent or praiseworthy--think about such things.

(Philippians 4:8, NIV)

Don't Lay on Your Son

During the night this woman's son died because she lay on him.

(1 Kings 3:19)

I N I Kɪɴɢs 3:19 we read a story of a woman who slept so carelessly on her new born son that he passed away before morning!

Are you carelessly sleeping on your God-given talents and gifts to the point they are dying or already dead? Most people who sleep on their gifts wake up later and become envious of those who have been nurturing and growing theirs.

> **Most people who sleep on their gifts wake up later and become envious of those who have been nurturing and growing theirs.**

How can we keep our gifts alive? How can we ensure they are increasing? By using and developing them. A lot of Christians have amazing gifts that they are not using; they have just put them to sleep and are laying on them. Some people don't use their gifts because they have despised them. They don't think they are significant. They envy other people's gifts not realizing God has a unique plan and task for everyone.

Is your gift crying out? I believe the baby must have cried out as the woman rolled and "lay on him," but she was too carried away to hear the cry of the baby. With care, feeding, and passion, the baby might have lived, grown-up like every other child, and brought his mother joy. His cries were ignored. He couldn't bear the weight of the woman for so long, and he gave up the ghost.

I pray in Jesus' name that every gift God has given you will be alive and strong. May God give you wisdom, understanding, and knowledge to use your gifts for His glory.

Big Things in Small Packs

He came to His own, and His own did not receive Him.

(John 1:11)

O NE OF THE reasons many people miss out on the blessings of God is that they do not recognise the value of the blessings being given to them. God usually packages very big things in small forms, and it's easy for proud people to miss them. If you are proud, you may look at the packaging of God's blessings and want nothing to do with them. You might say, "I am too much for this. This is definitely not the level I want to associate myself with." You do so not knowing that inside the pack are the answers to your present or future problems. Take our lord Jesus for example. He is the King of kings, but He didn't come to the earth as if He is.

One day, by the special grace of God, I had a revelation of what our Lord Jesus Christ looked like while He was on the earth. Indeed, nothing about His physical looks made me identify Him as a King. Isaiah 53:2 (NLT) is true:

My servant grew up in the Lord's presence like a tender green shoot, like a root in dry ground. There was nothing beautiful or majestic about his appearance, nothing to attract us to him.

Many despised Jesus because they did not believe anything good could ever come out of His hometown. When God packs majestic and glorious things in little parcels, the humble are well-placed to receive them.

Many people lose God's perfect will on choosing a life partner because they feel the person God is guiding them to do not match their standards. The people they reject are the ones God has prepared to be their present or future helpers. Some people have lost God-ordained friendships because they were not placed in shiny and attractive packages.

> **When God packs majestic and glorious things in little parcels, the humble are well-placed to receive them.**

Is God asking you to do something that looks small to you? God only gives good and perfect gifts and sometimes He puts great things in little packs. Humbly accept what God is giving you, and you will be amazed at the glory that will unfold from unravelling it.

Make Decisions from Your Desires

Enjoy what you have rather than desiring what you don't have. Just dreaming about nice things is meaningless—like chasing the wind.

(Ecclesiastes 6:9, NLT)

D REAMS AND DESIRES can only become a reality when there is action. To get the best, it is good to plan but better to act. "Decision prompts action, while desire only initiates dreams" (James Alo, *Vision Is a Decision*).

Remember faith without works is dead. A great dream, if not worked upon, is like having taps in the house through which no water flows.

Joseph's dream became a reality because of his acts of righteousness, perseverance, determination, and faithfulness. None of his God-given dreams might have come alive if he had unbelief, sin or timidity in his life.

The greatest limitation of a man is himself. When you conceptualize a plan, the next step is to get started. Once you begin, you will be on your way and making progress. John Mason said, "Shoot for the sky, if you miss it, you will land among the stars." So there must be shooting. "God goes with goers and moves with movers" (Reinhard Bonke). God doesn't work with those who only dream.

Have you wondered what Abraham's lot would have been if he had remained in his native land just dreaming of wonderful things but afraid to take a limb? He was indeed a man with a vision; that's why he could make a decision. What if Joseph had submitted to Potiphar's wife for fear of losing his job? He might have kept the job but attained nothing else—the master-servant of servants.

> **Sometimes what we think we are gaining by compromise is way below what we have lost by that compromise.**

Sometimes what we think we are gaining by compromise is way below what we have lost by that compromise. Joseph understood he needed righteousness to reach his God-given destiny.

What are the most important qualities you need to cultivate to achieve your purpose? King Solomon needed wisdom. It was one of the major qualities necessary for him to fulfill his purpose.

What do you major in? What are your strengths? What are your needs? Most job adverts specify the essential and desirable qualities needed to fulfil the role advertised. If you do not possess the essential qualities, it is unlikely you will be able to function properly in that role.

God who created us already knows our needs and has gifted us with the necessities to fulfil our destinies. The problem is the thief who works tirelessly to steal what God has deposited in us.

He is called the devil, and he has agents who help him. They are called demons.

Let us pray that God helps us cultivate these qualities and guard what He has given us jealously? Let us also pray that God helps us develop the qualities we need to fulfil our roles as virtuous women, great fathers, pastors, singers, writers, evangelists, etc. "The world is greatly blessed by people who do things, and not those who only talk about things." —John Mason.

Lazy people want more but get little but those who work hard will prosper. (Proverbs 13:4, NLT)

If you have a good dream in the night, ensure that by morning, you transform it into a vision by working on it. In conclusion, have great dreams and desires. Take decisions and actions. Pursue your vision!

Beating Procrastination

As long as it is day, we must do the works of him who sent me. Night is coming, when no one can work.

(John 9:4, NIV).

P ROCRASTINATION KEEPS TELLING you to do later what you could do earlier. It is a thief of time. Understanding how momentary and precious life is can help us in the battle against procrastination and time-wasting.

James 4:14b (NLT) says *"Your life is like the morning fog—it's here a little while, then it's gone."*

King David in Psalms 39:5 also said *"Indeed, You have made my days as handbreadths,*

And my age is as nothing before You; Certainly, every man at his best state is but vapor."

These scriptures should make us sober and indeed ask God for the grace to use the time we have fruitfully because it doesn't appear that we have an excess of it to waste.

But why do we procrastinate? Leading causes of procrastination include laziness, lack of motivation, poor time management and indecision. Procrastination is a form of passive disobedience.

> **To overcome procrastination, we need to put more effort into being organized and set achievable daily, monthly, and yearly targets.**

To overcome procrastination, we need to put more effort into being organized and set achievable daily, monthly, and yearly targets. Life for so many people is so busy that if you don't pen down certain things you want to achieve you might get overwhelmed with competing demands that you don't get to accomplish much. Also, put some effort into your time management, and if possible keep a log for a few days if you are not sure where all your time is going. Check your life to see if there are counterfeits things you end up doing whenever you want to do what you know you should be doing.

As Christians, we know that life is spiritual, so always commit your plans to God and ask for help to fulfil and exceed them according to His will. Pray to God to remove every appetite to engage in "time-stealing" activities. May God give us the grace to be fruitful in this precious gift of life in Jesus name.

Use Your Pain to Push

A woman giving birth to a child has pain because her time has come; but when her baby is born she forgets the anguish because of her joy that a child is born into the world.

(John 16:21, NIV)

ONE COOL EVENING around the time I was due to have my second child, I went for a long walk. A few minutes after returning home, I went into labour. As the labour progressed and went into the second phase as expected, I was having very strong and painful contractions. The midwives were monitoring the contractions electronically and whenever they saw them coming, they urged me to use the pain to push. They kept crying out, "Use the pain to push!"

In our lives, God may allow pain and use it as an instrument to birth our breakthroughs. In 1 Samuel Chapter 1, Hannah was going through severe pain inflicted by her husband's second wife.

And her rival also provoked her severely, to make her miserable, because the Lord had closed her womb. So it was, year by year, when she went up to the house of the Lord, that she provoked her; therefore she wept and did not eat. Then Elkanah her husband said to her, "Hannah, why do you weep? Why do you not eat? And why is your heart grieved? Am I not better to you than ten sons?

(1 Samuel 1:6-8)

Peninnah so provoked Hannah that she went into fasting. Hannah was desperate to have her child, and she refused to be comforted by her husband. Elkanah, Hannah's husband, loved her so much he never pressured her.

The second woman in the house was giving Hannah a miserable and consistent pain that drove her to make a vow to the Lord and cry desperately to God for a child. Her prayers were mercifully answered by God and a few months later, she delivered Samuel, one of the great prophets in the Bible.

Are you experiencing pain in your life? Use the pain to push! Make it an avenue to draw closer to God. Fix a regular time to pray and study God's Word. One songwriter says, "God has turned my misery into a ministry." That is exactly what God does. That "story" will be turned to glory. In Jesus' name.

In our lives, God may allow pain and use it as an instrument to birth our breakthroughs.

What You Do Have...

All praise to God, the Father of our Lord Jesus Christ, who has blessed us with every spiritual blessing in the heavenly realms because we are united with Christ.

(Ephesians 1:3)

W E MUST ALWAYS remind ourselves of what we have as Christians. This includes having the grace and abilities of a Spirit-filled child of God. Carefully read the following passage:

Now Peter and John went up together to the temple at the hour of prayer, the ninth hour. And a certain man lame from his mother's was carried, whom they laid daily at the gate of the temple which is called Beautiful, to ask alms from those who entered the temple; who, seeing Peter and John about to go into the temple, asked for alms. And fixing his eyes on him, with John, Peter said, "Look at us." So he gave them his attention, expecting to receive something from them. Then

*Peter said, "Silver and gold I do not have, **but what I do have I give you:** In the name of Jesus Christ of Nazareth, rise and walk." And he took him by the right hand and lifted him, and immediately his feet and ankle bones received strength. So he, leaping up, stood and walked and entered the temple with them—walking, leaping, and praising God. And all the people saw him walking and praising God. Then they knew that it was he who sat begging alms at the Beautiful Gate of the temple, and they were filled with wonder and amazement at what had happened to him.*

(Acts 3:1-10)

This story is simply amazing to me. We can learn several things from it, but I will highlight a few. Think about it; sometimes we moan about material things we don't have—money, food, clothes, etc., and we focus on these finished products. However, what we learn from this passage is that as Christians, we have the power that can create both seen and unseen things. This power has been freely given to us by our Lord Jesus Christ. The creative power within us far outweighs anything we will ever need. It was this same power that God used to create everything we see in our world today. When nothing existed, God spoke the word and things came into being.

> **The creative power within us far outweighs anything we will ever need.**

In the passage, Peter and John were saying to the sick man that they did not have money to give to him but had something far greater. They prayed for him and he got well. I am sure the sick man preferred to be healed than to be given $1 or $2, which he would have probably spent in a day or two and then continued begging.

The man in this story was blessed. He wasn't asked to choose between being healed and getting a few dollars. Peter and John did not give him any options. They just gave him what they knew was best for him. However, there may be circumstances when we need to choose between material possessions e.g. money, clothes, houses and something intangible like wisdom or God's anointing. What would you choose? It would be wise to choose the latter because, in the latter, you will find the former.

Seven Years of Plenty &
Seven Years of Famine

I must work the works of him that sent me, while it is day: the night cometh, when no man can work.

(John 9:4)

W HEN WE READ the scriptures, we understand something about God's ways. One thing we understand is that God created the day and night seasons. In life, we all have "nights" and "mornings." It is important to work in our "day" times because when our "nights" come we won't be able to work.

In Genesis 41, God gave Pharaoh a dream. In it, He warned there would be seven years of plenty and seven years of famine in the land of Egypt. Likewise, in our lives, there will be times of famine and times of plenty. What we do in times of plenty is very important. It will determine how the times of famine will look.

Like Pharaoh and Joseph, do we save and earn credits for the times of famine? Or do we just waste our resources in the times of plenty and lose hope in the times of famine?

What we do in times of plenty is very important. It will determine how the times of famine will look.

You might say, "Oh, I will never lack. I will always have enough." That might be true. But I am not only referring to material possessions or money. I am talking about the intangibles, the valuable things you can't touch: time, ideas, knowledge, experiences, and so forth.

As a youth, you have plenty of time and energy. How do you spend them? Sometimes we have many opportunities to reach out, preach the gospel, save some money, and give to the work of God. Do we spend these resources appropriately? Do we sow good seeds so we can reap later? Are we investing in prayers? Are we doing the work of Him who sent us while it is day?

The Beginning Gives an Impression

The end of a thing is better than its beginning.

(Ecclesiastes 7:8a)

T HE BEGINNING OF an event only gives an impression. It outlines your objectives and vision, showing what you hope to achieve. However, the end of that event provides the results. It reveals whether or not you have achieved your targets. Therefore, the end is the most important phase of an event.

There is a saying that "The journey of a thousand miles starts with a single step," so clearly, the beginning is good and essential. The problem occurs when we start a project without counting the cost or visualising where we want to end. That doesn't profit much.

On admission to a university, it is expected that after being a student for a few years, you will graduate and be certified in your field of study. However, if in the course of your studies you get distracted and careless, and you don't finish studying, you have only succeeded in giving people an impression.

Determination does not give birth to termination.

We can relate this to our Christians lives. As born-again Christians, our main goal is to make it to heaven. 1 Corinthians 15:19 says, "If in this life only we have hope in Christ, we are of all men the most pitiable." This means that as the children of God, our reward on the earth is not the target. So if for some reason—lust, pride or mere foolishness—we gradually expel ourselves from the race, we will suffer the consequences. The consequence of continuing in wilful sin is that the conclusion of your journey might not resemble the impression we gave at the beginning.

The beginning of the ministry God has given you, the great gift you manifest, and the wonderful fruit of the Spirit in your life creates a good impression, but sustenance will lead you to a good conclusion. An ideal way of not despising the days of little beginnings is to continue and improve on the little beginnings. When you start a good work, be determined to complete it in the best way. Determination does not give birth to termination.

I agree with Abraham Lincoln when he said, "Failure at the beginning is not really a failure, but failure at the end is the greatest failure.

Humility Brings Grace

True humility and fear of the Lord lead to riches, honour, and long life.

(Proverbs 22:4, NLT)

H UMILITY BRINGS GRACE, while pride leads to disgrace. Humility doesn't make you a fool; pride does. Consider the following scriptures:

When pride comes, then comes shame but with the humble is wisdom.

(Proverbs 11:2)

He (God) mocks proud mockers but gives grace to the humble.

(Proverbs 3:34)

Humility and the fear of God brings wealth, honour, and life.

(Proverbs 22:4)

All of you clothe yourselves with humility, towards one another, because God opposes the proud but gives grace to the humble. Humble yourselves therefore under God's mighty hand that he may lift you in due time.

(1 Peter 5:5b)

One of the symptoms of pride is not taking heed to Godly counsel. If you find it hard to take heed to Godly wisdom, it is likely you will miss messages from God because God sometimes speaks to us through people.

I see pride as a machine that lifts you high for the sole purpose of throwing you down from that height, so you can feel excruciating pain.

Humility is the key to lasting and constant promotion. When God releases a level of grace to us, and we are careful to give Him all the glory, the reward is more grace!

A man's pride brings him low, but a man of lowly spirit grows honour.

(Proverbs 29:30)

Now that we have mentioned the word "low" in the above verse, please be aware that humility is not the same as low self-esteem. Low self-esteem is associated with negative attributes like depression, underachievement, poor anger management (storing up anger and then exploding later), etc.

As Christians, we need to see ourselves through the lens of Christ Jesus. By His grace, we are:

- A chosen generation

- A royal priesthood

- A holy nation

- And God's special people that we may proclaim the praises of God who has called us out of darkness into His marvellous light (1 Peter 2:9, paraphrased).

From 1 Peter 2:9 and many other scriptures, we see there should be no room for low self-esteem in the life of a Christian. I usually remind myself I am too blessed to be depressed. Also, there should not be room for pride because, as we can see in 1 Peter 2:9, we have been chosen by God's mercy, not by our works or qualifications.

May God give us the grace to clothe ourselves with humility and confidence in Christ. In Jesus' name.

> **I see pride as a machine that lifts you high for the sole purpose of throwing you down from that height, so you can feel excruciating pain.**

Alternatives Distract

Trust in the Lord with all your heart, and lean not on your own understanding; In all your ways acknowledge Him, and He shall direct your paths.

(Proverbs 3:5-6)

W HEN THERE ARE many sticks in your matchbox, you might strike casually, but if you have one stick, you will strike meticulously. Our faith is sound and good when our hope is in God alone. When we recognise God as our only source, we will not be careless about our relationship with Him. Rather, we will take our prayer lives and service very seriously realising apart from Him, we can do nothing.

> *Now a woman, having a flow of blood for twelve years, who had spent all her livelihood on physicians and could not be healed by any, came from behind and touched the border of His garment. And immediately her flow of blood stopped.*
>
> (Luke 8:43-44)

In the above-cited verse, it seems the woman's total faith in Jesus was triggered by the fact that she had no help elsewhere. The Bible says she had spent her last penny on doctors in vain. She received no cure. Jesus was surely the only "stick in her matchbox."

God expects us to have faith and believe Him for everything in our lives. He says, "Cast all your cares upon me; I care for you." God can use people and circumstances to reach us, but we must recognise Him as the ultimate source and put our faith in Him. Sometimes we only turn back to God when the other sources our hearts are tuned to are closed.

To grow in faith, we must totally depend on God in all we do. Even though He may use teachers, doctors, friends, and other professionals to reach us, we must acknowledge God as the source. For without faith, it is impossible to please God. Abraham believed God, and it was accounted unto him as righteousness. He channelled his faith in the right direction; he believed God!

God can use people and circumstances to reach us, but we must recognise Him as the ultimate source and put our faith in Him.

You May Know More

I press on to reach the end of the race and receive the heavenly prize for which God, through Christ Jesus, is calling us.

(Philippians 3:14)

Every Christian who has received God's vision for his or her life may see it clearer than other people. Jesus knew His vision and mission perfectly well. That's why Peter, though his close friend and disciple, could not distract Him from His call. Peter knew Jesus is the Son of God. He knew He is the Saviour of the world. But at some point, he didn't know Jesus' mission was death on the cross. So in his ignorance, he tried to persuade Jesus not to die. However, Jesus rebuked him sternly saying, "Get behind me Satan!" Sometimes, people might be aware of your vision, but they may not understand your mission (what you have to do to get to your vision).

Many people have been greatly discouraged because of how negatively those close to and respected by them perceived their dreams and visions. They never got the encouragement they expected. If nobody encourages you to pursue your idea or vision, remember you are not the first. Many people were in your situation, but they still strived to succeed.

> *Now Joseph had a dream, and he told it to his brothers; and they hated him even more.*
>
> (Genesis 37:5)

> *Then he dreamed still another dream and told it to his brothers, and said, "Look, I have dreamed another dream. And this time, the sun, the moon, and the eleven stars bowed down to me." So he told it to his father and his brothers; and his father rebuked him and said to him, "What is this dream that you have dreamed? Shall your mother and I and your brothers indeed come to bow down to the earth before you?" And his brothers envied him, but his father kept the matter in mind.*
>
> (Genesis 37: 9-11)

Once a dream is made known, you are likely to encounter two sets of people:

1. Those who become jealous
2. Those who will keep your dream in mind

David had a similar experience when he had a burning zeal to fight for the people of God. This led him to ask questions about Goliath. In 1 Samuel 17:26, David asked, "What shall be done for the man who kills this Philistine and takes away the reproach from Israel? For who *is* this uncircumcised Philistine, that he should defy the armies of the living God?"

While David was speaking with the men, David's oldest brother Eliab retorted,

> *Why did you come down here? And with whom have you left those few sheep in the wilderness? I know your pride and the insolence of your heart, for you have come down to see the battle.*

(1 Samuel 17:28)

It takes a courageous yet humble mind to respond as David did to his brother Eliab's harsh words. Verses 29 and 30 (NLT) reads: …"What have I done now?", David replied, "I was only asking a question!" He walked over to some others and asked them the same thing and received the same answer.

David was very wise and was not interested in pleasing men more than God. His brothers were not with him in the field when he saved the lambs from the mouths of bears. They were not present when he delivered his flock from the lions. So when he was asking for the reward for killing Goliath, he sounded ridiculous and awkward.

> **If you are not being encouraged by others, follow David's example: encourage yourself and move forward.**

Most people who are not witnesses to the victories of your past will not have confidence in your current visions or abilities. When Saul met Jesus and was converted to Paul the Apostle, the other disciples were astonished and scared. At first, they did not believe his confession. Of course, they were not with him when he met Jesus, so it was difficult for them to understand his mission.

If you are not being encouraged by others, follow David's example: encourage yourself and move forward. Accept the encouragement you get, if any. Ignore the discouragements. Rebuke temptations and embrace confirmations as you pursue your vision.

Minding the Weather?

The lazy man will not plow because of winter; He will beg during harvest and have nothing.

(Proverbs 20:4)

A LAZY MAN WILL always find a reason not to do what he is supposed to. Proverbs 22:13 puts it this way: "The sluggard says, 'There is a lion outside! Or I shall be slain in the streets.'"

If you mind the weather, you might get nothing done. Most people who finished great work did not have an excellent start or smooth process. The fear of "What might happen if I...?" "What will they say if I...?" "How will they see it if I...?" "What will they do if I...?" has stopped great minds from accomplishing significant feats.

Imagine how the lazy man in Proverbs 22:13 exaggerated what might happen to him if he went to work. He said: "There is a lion outside." I wonder if the lion was assigned to kill him or if it had eaten up the other people who went out for the day's work.

The sluggard looked for a big reason to satisfy his conscience and then he covered up to sleep. A lazy person always finds excuses not to work. The sluggard must understand that the so-called "lions" and "murderers" will never leave the streets. Therefore, if he is planning to go out only when they are gone, he never will.

Obstacles will always be in your life. Attackers, whether in the form of people or things, will always exist. Morale killers or "murderers" are constantly out there.

The absence of electrical power is no reason to cancel a night's study, especially if power failures are common in the area you live. Being unemployed is no reason to be jobless. Find something good to do. Keep busy, so you do not become a busybody.

Yielding to the guidance of the Holy Spirit is a great way to live an efficient and fruitful life.

You will always find a reason not to do what you don't want to. The old adage says, "When there is a will, there is a way." So when "there is no will, there is no way." If you desire to do something, decide to do it. If you desire to be holy, decide to be holy and ask the Holy Spirit for help. If you desire to be hard working, decide to be.

In life, there is power in determination. You will be very surprised how determination can help you break through many barriers. If you move to slowly, you might be tempted to look at everything on your journey, including the irrelevant things and you might not meet your target. If you move too "fast," meaning you are running with zeal without knowledge, you might bypass a treasure you should have picked up.

Yielding to the guidance of the Holy Spirit is a great way to live an efficient and fruitful life. God is looking out for your efforts because He wants to bless them.

Purpose of Persecution

For he knows the ways that I take; when he has tested me, I shall come forth as gold.

(Job 23:10)

M OST CHRISTIANS WHOM God will use to affect their generation will be persecuted. This might be as a result of the refining process.

It seems as if the days of persecution from the world are over. However, we must be careful, it is not the hunger to live right and do God's perfect will that is fast vanishing.

In fact, everyone who wants to live a godly life will be persecuted.

(2 Timothy 3:12, NLT)

As Christians, when we say we have not experienced persecution, it might just be that we have not tried living godly lives. Faced with persecution, David cried out for help:

Help, O Lord, for the godly are fast disappearing!
The faithful have vanished from the earth!

(Psalm 12:1, NLT)

Jesus did not promise Christians trouble-free lives, but He promised us overcoming, conquering, and victorious lives. He also promised us the Comforter. If there is no sorrow, grief or suffering, why would we need a comforter? The Comforter (the Holy Spirit) goes into the fire with us and makes sure we are not burnt. The experience of the three Hebrew men in the book of Daniel is evidence of this:

> *Then these men were bound in their coats, their trousers, their turbans, and their other garments, and were cast into the midst of the burning fiery furnace. Therefore, because the king's command was urgent, and the furnace exceedingly hot, the flame of the fire killed those men who took up Shadrach, Meshach, and Abed-Nego. And these three men, Shadrach, Meshach, and Abed-Nego, fell down bound into the midst of the burning fiery furnace. Then King Nebuchadnezzar was astonished, and he rose in haste and spoke, saying to his counsellors, "Did we not cast three men bound into the midst of the fire?" They answered and said to the king, "True, O king." "Look!" he answered, "I see four men loose, walking in the midst of the fire; and they are not hurt, and the form of the fourth is like the Son of God." Then Nebuchadnezzar went near the mouth of the burning fiery furnace and spoke, saying,*

"Shadrach, Meshach, and Abed-Nego, servants of the Most High God, come out, and come here." Then Shadrach, Meshach, and Abed-Nego came from the midst of the fire.

(Daniel 3:21-26)

Praise God!

If God allows a trail of your faith and you go through it without compromise, then a promotion awaits you on the other side!

God's presence in a believer's life makes the difference. God will make the difference between those who serve Him and those who do not. Remember the story of Moses and the burning bush (Exodus Chapter 3). Moses witnessed that although the bush was on fire, it was not being consumed. Likewise, fire might be present in your life, but you won't get burnt.

> **If God allows a trail of your faith and you go through it without compromise, then a promotion awaits you on the other side!**

Sometimes God uses tough circumstances to create tough people. The excellent news about the trying times believers face is they cannot be compared to the glory that will be revealed later (if the suffering is indeed for Christ).

For our light affliction, which is but for a moment, is working for us a far more exceeding and eternal weight of glory, while we do not look at the things which are seen, but at the things which are not seen. For the things which are seen are temporary, but the things which are not seen are eternal.

(2 Corinthians 4:17-18)

The greatest need of a Christian who is passing through a refining process is faith. Faith is seeing the unseen, recognising the glory ahead and rejoicing in it.

Therefore do not cast away your confidence, which has a great reward. For you have need of endurance, so that after you have done the will of God, you may receive the promise:"For yet a little while, And He who is coming will come and will not tarry". Now the just shall live by faith; But if anyone draws back, My soul has no pleasure in him. But we are not of those who draw back to perdition, but of those who believe to the saving of the soul.

(Hebrews 10:35-39)

Believers who do not focus on the unseen give up when their victory and glory is near. Of course, this is when trouble seems to be at its greatest.

Enemies and Critics Play a Role

The LORD says to my Lord: "Sit at My right hand until I make Your enemies a footstool for Your feet."

(Psalm 110:1)

I DISCOVERED THAT AT times, God uses our "close enemies" to transport us to our God-given destinies. Consider these examples: the almighty God used the Pharisees to accomplish and fulfil the ministry of Jesus on the cross. God used Joseph's brothers to fulfil his God-given dreams. Though they meant him harm, God harmoniously turned everything around for good.

Little will your enemies know that all their schemes will be turned around for your glory. As long as you are steadfast in prayer and doing the will of God, any attack of the Enemy that seems to have succeeded against you is only a blessing in disguise. Soon, the glory will be revealed. No wonder Paul said in 2 Corinthians 4:17,

*For our light affliction, which is but for a moment,
is working for us a far more exceeding and eternal
weight of glory.*

This does not mean that the offenders will not receive their punishment. Joseph's brothers were chastised by God for their cruelty toward Joseph. Judas Iscariot, who betrayed Jesus, was punished. The Bible says it would have been better if he wasn't born (Matthew 26:24).

Little will your enemies know that all their schemes will be turned around for your glory.

Enemies can be very childish and ignorant; they may not even have a clear knowledge of what they want or what they are doing. Jesus said on the cross, "Lord forgive them for they do not know what they do." Jesus also said we should pray for our enemies.

The Enemy's plan and intention can never succeed against God's plan when we are steadfast in prayer and have a sound relationship with God. Do you remember how God used Goliath (an enemy) to expose David and bring him to greatness? We do not always get to our goals and destinies through friends alone. Sometimes our enemies play an important role.

Why Advertise Your Problems?

That you may keep discretion, and your lips may guard knowledge.

(Proverbs 5:2)

P ROBLEMS ARE TO be solved, not bought. So why advertise them? Over the years, I have learned not to share my challenges indiscriminately. When you have a need or you're facing a challenge, what you need is a solution, not sympathy. If you indiscriminately share your challenges, you might fall into the hands of a gifted pessimist. This person is likely to increase your fears, reduce your faith, and greatly sympathise with you. Don't waste your time. Be wise. Be objective.

I am not advising you to be secretive but to be discrete. Trust God to direct you to those you should talk to and steer you away from those you should not. Let us take an example from the Shunamite woman in 2 Kings 4:8-9. She refused to be distracted. She was tight-lipped about her problem until she met the right person to solve it. Her son had just died. Yet, she said, "It is well" in answer to those who asked what her problem was. If she had opened up to all those who asked her if all was well, she might never have found a solution. Perhaps their pessimistic outlook might have discouraged her from getting to the man of God. Or they would have encouraged her to accept the situation as it was.

Another lesson to learn from this story is the fact that a God-given gift doesn't mean a trouble-free, challenge-free or problem-free gift. God miraculously gave her a son but at some point, the son died. The devil wanted to spoil her testimony but thank God for this woman of faith!

Trust God to direct you to those you should talk to and steer you away from those you should not.

I made up my mind that those who share their challenges with me should get something from me. If I can't help materially or morally, then I can surely help spiritually. I can pray about the situation. As Christians, we are never empty. Peter and John helped the crippled man at the Beautiful Gate as recorded in Acts 3:1-9. The physically challenged man was expecting something material but received a supernatural gift in the name of Jesus.

And fixing his eyes on him, with John, Peter said, "Look at us." 5 So he gave them his attention, expecting to receive something from them. 6 Then Peter said, "Silver and gold I do not have, but what I do have I give you: In the name of Jesus Christ of Nazareth, rise up and walk." (Acts 3:4-6)

Indeed, the man got his healing and began praising God. Another thing to learn from this passage is that many times, we expect less than what God intends to give to us. On this day, the crippled man was only expecting money from the anointed men of God when he could have gotten a lot more—his sight!

God does not only want to give us temporary gladness or breakthroughs. He does not intend to give us just "money" that will get us nowhere after a short time. He has every intention to give us total freedom and lead us to eternal glory. The money would have only satisfied the lame man for a short while, but his healing was the ultimate gift. I hope you get the message.

Problems are to be solved not bought so why advertise them? Aim to be a solution, not just a sympathiser. We are gods. Let us be in the business of correcting wrongs wherever we go.

Wisdom Overtakes Strength

*The wise are mightier than the strong, and those
with knowledge grow stronger and stronger.*

(Proverbs 24:5, NLT)

W ISDOM HAVE DELIVERED many people from unnecessary
fights, quarrels, and trouble. When the Pharisees wanted
to tempt Jesus Christ as recorded in Luke 20:20-26 (NLT),
something interesting happened. Read this:

> *Keeping a close watch on him; they sent spies,
> who pretended, to be honest. They hoped to catch
> Jesus in something he said so that they might
> hand him over to the power and authority of the
> governor. So the spies questioned him, "Teacher,
> we know that you speak and teach what is right
> and that you do not show partiality and teach the
> way of God by the truth. Is it right for us to pay
> taxes to Caesar or not?*

When you get to the stage in your life where your focus and commitment becomes offensive to others, it could be a sign you are on the right track. At that point, the world hunts you down to tempt you.

In the passage above, Jesus answered those spies by saying, "Show me a denarius. Whose portrait and inscription are on it? "Caesar's" they replied. He said to them, "Then give to Caesar what is Caesar's and to God what is God's." They were unable to trap Jesus with what He said in public. Astonished by His answer, they became silent. Thank God!

One of the elements of divine wisdom is discernment. Jesus has the spirit of wisdom (Isaiah 11:2). Therefore, when they tried to catch Him with His words, they could not. So they pretended to be nice and applauding. But Jesus saw right through them. He discerned their evil plan.

Isaiah prophesied about Jesus' ability to discern. In Isaiah 11:3 the Bible says, "*He will delight in obeying the Lord. He will never judge by appearance, false evidence or hearsay.*" The wise King Solomon could also discern. We see this in the story of the two prostitutes dragging over a baby. King Solomon because of his wisdom discerned the truth from a lie, so he couldn't be tricked. Wisdom indeed overtakes strength.

> **They were unable to trap Jesus with what He said in public. Astonished by His answer, they became silent.**

Revenge Only Shows "Equality"

Repay no one evil for evil. Have regard for good things in the sight of all men.

(Romans 12:17)

W HEN YOU SEEK to avenge a wrong, it proves one key thing: you are similar to the offender. People on the same level act alike. "Forgive, that's the last thing your enemies want you to do" (John Mason).

When you seek revenge, it clearly shows:

1. You are on the same level as your offender

2. You do not trust God to avenge your case

3. You probably don't think God is capable of giving justice

"What are you doing more than others?" Jesus asked that profound question in Matthew 5:47. How can we do more than others? By loving when they hate, praying when they curse, and greeting when they are resentful.

And if you greet only your brothers, what are you doing more than others"? Do not even pagans do that? Be ye perfect therefore as your heavenly Father is perfect.

(Matthew 5:47-48)

A wise man knows how to forgive believing his God can take care of every situation. If you take revenge, you have received your reward.

When you are hurt, you need healing, not weapons to fight back. You might only sustain further injuries. God heals all kinds of wounds: emotional, physical, and spiritual.

Taking revenge is a sin. Therefore, it is foolish to let your offender offer you two wrongs: hurt and death, knowing sin leads to death. There is power in forgiveness.

It is a dreadful thing for an unrepentant offender to fall into the hands of God. However, when an offender falls into your hands, how far can you go? If you commit them to God's hand, that settles the matter. Do not try to do God's job. He said: "Vengeance is mine; I will repay."

> **When you are hurt, you need healing, not weapons to fight back.**

Handling Success and Challenges

No, dear brothers and sisters, I have not achieved it, but I focus on this one thing: Forgetting the past and looking forward to what lies ahead.

(Philippians 3:13)

I F YOU SUCCEED, you might be impressed. If you think you failed, don't give into depression. In whatever case, press on.

Stopping after a great success or achievement is an error. Those who look at yesterday's achievements and see them as "very great" have not grown at all. When you stop trying to press further, it means you have stopped succeeding. Real winners never give up whether they experience successes or failures. Instead, they keep pushing forward and looking for different ways to achieve their goals. Success is continuous, and successful minds never stop trying.

If you succeed at one level, don't stop there. Move on! Aim for a higher level. Apostle Paul, an example of a person who succeeded in his ministry said:

I press on towards the goal, to win the prize for which God has called me heavenward in Christ Jesus.

(Philippians 3:14)

If God promised to crown our efforts with success, we must continuously go after greater success. On the other hand, failure may have an automatic depressing effect. Have you ever experienced failure? I have. One experience that readily comes to my mind happened when I was a teenager in teens' church. I was chosen to represent my church in a teenage Sunday school competition against other churches. My church parish was the headquarters for the other competing parishes. Therefore, the expectations were high.As it turned out, when the competition was over, we came last. Wow! I felt sad. I almost vowed never to enter a competition again. I did not even want to go to church anymore. But after a while, I forgot about the whole experience and picked myself up. Sometime later, when I was in the adult Sunday school, there was another Sunday school competition. This time, the parish I attended was small in size. I braced myself to represent my church again. This time, we came first. The experience was positive and very rewarding! With a good attitude, you will always gain something from every trial!

Keep pushing and moving forward no matter what. If you never fail, you might not appreciate success. Ignorance keeps a man down after a failure. John Mason said, "If you fall, pick something up." I add to that by saying, "If you fall, pick something up and move forward."

Whether you fail or succeed, keep pressing on. Make sure you have a vision you can die for. Someone once said, "If you have

NOTHING ORDINARY ABOUT YOU

not found something you can die for, you may die for nothing." Staying close to great people alone doesn't automatically make you great. Otherwise, men like Gehazi and Judas, who were close to Elisha and Jesus

Whether you fail or succeed, keep pressing on.

respectively, would have been great. Vision is the watchword! So you must stay close to great people but also catch their vision— see things the way they do.

Note: It's not only failure that can stop a man. Success can also have a negative effect. The remedy is to be relentless. Have a continuous determination to press further.

Every Second Is a Seed

Making the best use of the time, because the days are evil.

(Ephesians 5:16, ESV)

Every day comes with something, so take something out of every day, for no day comes with nothing.

E VERY DAY COMES with a gift but some people do not receive it. Irrespective of the big plans you have for tomorrow, do not despise today. Whenever you have the opportunity to see a new day, make sure you do not live it at yesterday's level. An excellent way to grow is to avoid repeating the mistakes of yesterday.

Whatever condition today seems to be presenting, there is something worthwhile a wise man can do. Make use of every opportunity to do something right and good. Even if, for some reason, you are locked indoors and can't step out of the house, use it as an opportunity to pray behind closed doors. Let nothing stop you from doing good. Choose to be unstoppable. Every day has something to offer.

Paul and Silas are examples of people who choose to be unstoppable when thrown into prison. They were bound in prison and couldn't lay hands on the sick or stand and preach. But their mouths were not tied, so they sang and prayed.

> *About midnight, Paul and Silas were praying and singing hymns to God and the other prisoners were listening to them. Suddenly, there was such a violent earthquake that the foundations of the prison were shaken. At once, all the prison doors flew open, and everybody's chain came loose.*
>
> (Acts 16:25-27)

Whenever you feel restricted or constrained to a particular area, be fully engaged in what you can do, and you will find liberty. When you make use of what you have where you are, God will rise to honour you. No matter the prison you are in now, make sure you still find something good to do. Remember how Joseph the dreamer was still doing good in all the "prisons" he went to. His conduct soon lifted him from prison to power. If nothing else, a day has 24 hours to offer; find something good to do in it.

Whenever you feel restricted or constrained to a particular area, be fully engaged in what you can do, and you will find liberty.

Every second is a seed. One of the greatest opportunities a day can offer is someone to help.

> *Do not say to your neighbour come back later; I will give it tomorrow when you now have it with you.*
>
> (Proverbs 3:28)

Sow good seeds and sow them in time. Some of the things we are reaping today are what we sowed yesterday. Whatever we sow today, we will reap tomorrow. Every second is a seed.

Called to be Separate

Therefore, come out from their midst and be separate," says the Lord. "And do not touch what is unclean; and I will welcome you.

(2 Corinthians 6:17)

D URING MY LATE teenage years, I started experiencing separation from close friends and cliques. Initially, I was worried because it was not a deliberate act. I just noticed I was no longer at ease with certain company. My perception, thinking, and lifestyle were becoming different from theirs. All this was happening as I decided to follow Christ and draw closer to Him.

Separation is one of the first and most vital steps to success. You must see the way of the Lord before you walk in it but to see His way, you must be separated. That will require leaving some people or things you were comfortable with behind. Every person who is called to greatness must experience separation—deliberately or not.

If you are walking in God's ways, do not expect everyone to understand you.

God commanded Abraham to leave his father's native land. It was only when he took the first step in obedience that his journey of greatness began. God separated Joseph from his brothers and fulfilled His purpose for him. God separated David in the wilderness and prepared him for success there.

Even among the Christian fold, some people will experience separation. This is because while others are doing the "normal" or "ordinary things," the anointing of God on their lives will cause them to function differently, thus, leading to separation.

Our ways are not God's ways neither are His thoughts our thoughts.

(Isaiah 55:8)

When we decide to work as God desires, people think we are strange. That's because we deviate from the "normal." God showed Moses His ways and acts to the children of Israel. Moses walked in God's ways and many times, the children of Israel could not understand him. If you are walking in God's ways, do not expect everyone to understand you. When God reveals His way of faith, divine giving and sacrifice, godly love, sincere speech, patience, humility, and righteousness, you will be a lamb amid wolves—strikingly different.

When these separations happen, and you can't find yourself in others, you may be tempted to conform to the normal standards. However, you are not called to conform to the world's standards. You are called to be separate and show others God's way.

In regard to these, they think it strange that you do not run with them in the same flood of dissipation, speaking evil of you.

(1 Peter 4:4)

Never forget you are a citizen of heaven living on the earth. Keep your identity as a chosen one of God.

Grace for the Race

Let us then approach the throne of grace with confidence, so that we may receive mercy and find grace to help us in our time of need.

(Hebrews 4:16)

EVERY CHRISTIAN NEEDS the grace of God. It is a major spiritual asset. If we must differentiate ourselves from the ordinary and operate extraordinarily, we need the grace of God in our lives. It is possible your siblings all inherited dullness of the brain. However, being a child of God qualifies you to receive the special grace of God that can make you brilliant. Your family might have ailments that are inherited but if you are a child of God, the grace of God can deliver you from them. A specific pattern of sin may exist in your family but as a child of God, you can overcome it because you have access to the grace of God in great measure.

The question then is, "What is the grace of God?" Many have said it is the unmerited or undeserved favour and mercy of God shown to man. Yes, I believe it is. So when God talks about the lawful captives being set free, it is His grace that will perform it. Grace, in my opinion, is also a divine access to rare treasures and abilities you would ordinarily not have.

> **Grace, in my opinion, is also a divine access to rare treasures and abilities you would ordinarily not have.**

Remember, the earnest expectation of the creature awaits the manifestation of the sons of God. We can only manifest when we obtain this divine ability. No wonder in most of Paul's opening prayers, he asked for the grace of God before anything else.

As you seek to know God more in your walk with Him, may the grace of our Lord Jesus Christ be with you this season and always. In Jesus' name. Amen!

Kind Evils

People may cover their hatred with pleasant words, but they're deceiving you.

(Proverbs 26:24)

I T SOUNDS LIKE an oxymoron; how can evil be kind? Yes, unfortunately, many evils appear good to people. Hence, they do not think it is evil in the first place.

But I am not surprised! Even Satan disguises himself as an angel of light.

(2 Corinthians 11:14)

The devil can use seemingly kind deeds, kind words, and kind people to distract us from our destinies and missions. Not all that glitters is gold and temptations are usually subtle. You need discernment to detect if an offer is the will of God for you.

A woman may gradually fall into adultery if she finds a man who seems to care for her more than her husband. Truly, this man may be very nice but is that a reason to commit adultery? Adultery gets you speedily into hell. It can cause you to lose your home and destiny, so is that little kindness worth the great pain you will suffer?

A sad story to consider is that of the young and old prophets in 1 Kings Chapter 13. The old prophet lied to the young prophet saying he was led to tell him to come back to the town and have a meal in his house. On its own, the gesture sounded hospitable and kind. However, if you read the full story, you will realize the young prophet would have been better off sleeping under the tree. He was deceived by the old prophet, disobeyed God and unfortunately, a lion killed him.

The devil can use seemingly kind deeds, kind words, and kind people to distract us from our destinies and missions.

Only God gives good and perfect gifts. If the devil offers you something, rest assured he expects you to give him back something incomparable to what he offered you. Somebody once said that the devil offers sinful pleasures but always hides the price tag. As for our God, His love is unconditional. He loves us sincerely and dearly as His children. That is why we say our God is good, all the time.

No Civilian Life

Be sober, be vigilant; because your adversary the devil walks about like a roaring lion, seeking whom he may devour.

(1 Peter 5:8)

A s Christians, we have been called to live a military kind of life. Military life is generally characterized by a high level of discipline and readiness. When duty calls, you are expected to report immediately and perform the task. Obedience is paramount and there is no room for lazing around. You have signed up for something important and other people's lives depend on you.

To perform their duties, soldiers are usually given authority. Growing up in a military home, I saw first-hand the discipline and authority military personnel are expected to exhibit.

> *Soldiers don't get tied up with civilian life, for then they cannot please the officer who enlisted them.*
>
> (2 Timothy 2:4, NLT)

The NASB translation of the above passage reads,

> *No soldier in active service entangles himself in the affairs of everyday life, so that he may please the one who enlisted him as a soldier.*
>
> (2 Timothy 2:4)

As children of God, we are called to be soldiers, but they are "civilians" out there who do not want us to please God, the one who enlisted us. In practice, these "civilian" distractions can include things like gossip, gluttony, excessive watching of movies, excessive use of social media and anything that distract us and keep us away from our calling. Real soldiers do not compromise. They are alert, strong, and decisive.

In practice, these "civilian" distractions can include things like gossip, gluttony, excessive watching of movies, excessive use of social media and anything that distract us and keep us away from our calling.

Also, God has given Christian soldiers—both male and female—the grace, authority, and anointing to live as a soldier does with discipline and working righteousness. He has given us the strength and willingness to do God's work and will.

As we release ourselves to God's grace and obey that still small voice, we will find ourselves soaring above the civilian affairs of this world.

Wisdom: What Does It Offer?

Wisdom is the principal thing; therefore get wisdom. And in all your getting, get understanding.

(Proverbs 4:7)

THE NIV VERSION puts it this way: "Wisdom is supreme." The word "supreme" is defined as "most important, greatest, and most intense."

Wisdom is indeed the principal thing for everyone who wants success in life. Any person, ministry, body or organisation lacking wisdom will always be far from perfection. Lots of deficiencies will be present irrespective of its potential and efforts.

Wisdom is the principal thing; it brings promotion, honour, grace, and glory (Proverbs 4: 8-9). Wisdom is the principal thing (most important thing) because in its absence, your efforts and resources can be wasted. This is so despite the power, strength, and potential you may have. For example, someone who laboured hard and finally received a financial breakthrough but had no wisdom to manage the funds. Very soon, all the money will be gone and that person will be back to square one. Or someone who fasts for many days, sacrificing lots of pleasures but is tempted after the fast and falls cheaply on the laps of anger, rage or gossip. Due to a lack of wisdom, that person leaks all the anointing gathered while fasting.

Wisdom has been the principal thing from creation.

> *The Lord formed me from the beginning before he created anything else. I was appointed in ages past, at the very first, before the earth began.*
>
> (Proverbs 8:22-23)

God had to call forth wisdom before creating the oceans, hills, mountains, clouds, and sea boundaries. This speaks to the importance of seeking wisdom first before anything else.

In Proverbs 8:30, wisdom still speaking says,

> *Then I was beside Him as a master craftsman; And I was daily His delight, rejoicing always before Him.*

If God needed wisdom so much to craft creation, what other projects, establishments or programs would survive without it?

Practical Ways to Obtain Wisdom

1. First, give your life to Christ. He is the wisdom of God (1 Corinthians 1:24).

2. If you are born again, you can continually ask God to increase your wisdom (James 1:5).

3. Seek godly counsel with God's leading.

4. Study the Word of God.

Life is too short to make lots of mistakes. A common definition of wisdom says "Wisdom is the application of knowledge." This is true but sometimes the "knowledge" that needs to be applied is "God's divine knowledge," not only the type you find in ordinary books or

> **Wisdom also helps us overcome temptations and avoid deception.**

through standard research. For example, like Isaac in Genesis Chapt 26, you might know there is a famine in a land.

The application of earthly wisdom would be to leave the barren land and move to somewhere fruitful. That is just common sense really. However, in Genesis Chapter 26, God instructed Isaac to do what seemed senseless. He told him to stay in the land of famine. Isaac knew God's will and obeyed it. He remained in that dry land, and God blessed him right there. Our God is a miracle-working God; let us never forget that!

Wisdom also helps us overcome temptations and avoid deception. In Matthew 4:1-11, the devil tempted Jesus in the wilderness using adulterated scriptures. But Jesus knew the true Word of God and was empowered to overcome the devil by the Word.

Also, when the hypocrites wanted to tempt Jesus in Luke 20:23-25, asking Him if they should pay taxes to Caesar or not, Jesus could discern their motives. They hoped to trap Him with their question but by the Spirit of God, Jesus gave them a wise answer:

Show me a denarius. Whose image and inscription does it have?" They answered and said, "Caesar's." And He said to them, "Render therefore to Caesar the things that are Caesar's and to God the things that are God's.

(Luke 20:24-25)

The denarius (coin) had Caesar's image and inscription on it, so Jesus said to give it to Caesar! We are made in God's image and His Word is inscribed in our hearts. Therefore, we belong to God, and we give ourselves to Him. What wisdom!

Here is a little summary: wisdom is the principal thing. We can increase in godly wisdom by being born again, praying, studying God's Word, reading godly materials, and receiving godly counsel through the generous gifts of the Holy Spirit.

Remain a David

When pride comes, then comes shame; but with the humble is wisdom.

(Proverbs 11:2)

M ANY PEOPLE THINK Saul fell because he had an evil heart right from the start, and he wasn't a good man. However, when you read through Scripture, you see that wasn't the case. Initially, Saul was like David. Read 1 Samuel 9:21. It took a series of events for him to transform into the Saul who ended up being friendly with a witch.

Most people are like David when they are first called by God. However, their responses to challenging times will determine whether they remain like David in humility and obedience or take on Saul's character. The ministerial journey involves promotion, victory, the gathering of experiences, anointing, authority and more. If we are not careful, we can become proud and envious

> **When pride and envy are fed, they fuel rebellion; where rebellion remains, rejection is inevitable.**

thinking we can earn the gifts on our own. When pride and envy are fed, they fuel rebellion; where rebellion remains, rejection is inevitable.

To remain Davids, we have to continually humble ourselves before God and godly authorities. We must also focus on God rather than people and be obedient to God every step of the way. Trust in God and His orders, not on your understanding or experiences. Sincerely confess and repent of your sins whenever you go wrong and are chastised.

Neutral = A Big Negative

Whoever is not with me is against me, and whoever does not gather with me scatters.

(Matthew 12:30, ESV)

I F YOU ARE a child of God, you cannot afford to be neutral. In other words, you have to pick a side. Life is a battlefield. Whose army are you in? In God's kingdom, there is no room for spectators. If you have been surviving in that mode as a Christian, it is time to wake up. Maybe you have been on probation. But the fact that you are reading this book at this time is another reminder to get up and stay active.

The signs of lukewarmness according to Revelations 3:18 are finding "comfort in nothing," claiming "all is well," not doing anything about pressing circumstances and being negligent and complacent about the work of God. When people want to become lukewarm, they convince themselves they have everything working for them. They have riches and comfort and lack nothing. To that effect, they say to themselves, "I don't have to do anything extra. I don't have to disturb the devil. Let him be, and I will be. I will just live a normal life and fit into any circumstance. When I am in 'Rome' I can do as the Romans do."

We are not saved to be lukewarm. Lukewarmness is not neutral; it's a serious condition and big negative. It's a minus to God's kingdom. The Bible says the harvest is ripe but the labourers are few. The remedy for lukewarmness is to be zealous and repent. This is according to Revelations 3:19. Some Christians do not see any reason to be zealous for God. They get saved and that's it. They stop at that level with no desire to be baptised, to evangelise or be a part of the work of God.

God loves active people. He is not impressed by laziness. Apostle Paul was a very active and zealous man. Even though his energy was initially being channelled against God, God arrested him and used him mightily. Paul's zeal and energy were used to impact the world for Christ.

Zeal has a lot to do with your will. God will not force anyone to be zealous. The Holy Spirit can and will always give grace, but it is really in our hands to get

The remedy for lukewarmness is to be zealous and repent.

up and work. If you want to be relevant in the business of God's work, you can't have idle hands. "When you joyfully do little things like they are big things, then God will do big things like they are little things" (Debby and Bob Gas). The key is to stay relevant in God's work.

Listen to Yourself

Well then, if you teach others, why don't you teach yourself? You tell others not to steal, but do you steal?

(Romans 2:21, NLT)

A s Christians, sometimes we fall into the same temptation we warn others and write about or rebuke others for. That's why you should digest your message before you preach it. I was watching a video by Bishop T.D Jakes. I think he was ministering to church leaders, preachers, and pastors. He said something very striking. I will paraphrase it,

> Most preachers are better at serving than at eating, just as most chefs are better professionals at cooking than serving. They only pop biscuits into their mouths now and then, but they don't eat right. Sometimes the people they serve eat better than them. They become such professionals at giving that they lose the ability to receive. The result is that over time, leaders can become

> spiritually depleted and fall into sin: affairs, lust, and perversion. They don't even know how they got there, but they got there through malnutrition.

When God gives you a message, make sure you take it in. Ask God sincerely for the grace to apply the word to your life. Most preachers think they are only called to serve and teach, not to learn. The devil will try to attack you with what you have preached.

Some people prefer to say the right thing than to do it but there are dangers in walking that path. John the Baptist, after announcing Jesus as the Messiah and leading many to believe (John 1:29-37), soon became doubtful. This great preacher turned around and asked if Jesus was the Saviour or if he should expect someone else (Luke 7:20). I wonder what transpired between the time John was so sure Jesus was the Son of God and the time he began to doubt. Can the truth change?

> **When God gives you a message, make sure you take it in. Ask God sincerely for the grace to apply the word to your life.**

Situations can change; culture can change; trends can change but the truth of God's Word cannot change. It is a settled matter. Sometimes we question truths that were previously revealed to us, and we were convinced about.

Thank God for His mercies and grace for repentance when we err. But we can avoid more temptations if we read our writings, counsel our own marriages the way we counsel others, and listen to the messages we preach to others. The truth is we are just messengers, so the messages we share are not ours but God's. Therefore, the messengers must partake in the eating. No wonder some end up not being recognised; we won't be judged mainly by what we serve but what we do. Jesus said:

> *Not everyone who says to Me, Lord! Lord! Shall enter the kingdom of Heaven, but he who does the will of My Father in Heaven. Many will say to Me on that day, Lord! Lord! Did we not prophesy in Your name, and through Your name throw out demons, and through Your name do many wonderful works? And then I will say to them I never knew you! Depart from Me, those working lawlessness!*
>
> (Matthew 7:21-23)

The problem with the people Jesus spoke about in the preceding verse is they thought they would earn credits by only telling others what to do. They did not think it was necessary to look inward and examine themselves.

God wants us to be zealous about His work, and He rewards diligent service. But even more, He wants a genuine relationship with us and obedience to Him in our daily lives.

If You Can't Control Your Mouth, You Can't Control Your Life

He who keeps his mouth keeps his life; he who opens his lips wide, it is ruin to him.

(Proverbs 13:3)

MANY SCRIPTURES DRAW a connection between the words we speak and the quality of life we live.

Do you see a man hasty in his words? There is more hope for a fool than for him.

(Proverbs 29:20)

A man's words have a direct influence on his life. The power of life and death lies in the tongue (Proverbs 18:21). What we utter with our mouths comes back to us and affects our lives positively or negatively. So we have to give thought to what we say to ourselves and others.

When it comes to controlling the tongue, one good place to start is guarding the heart and meditating on the Word of

God. This reveals God's perspective of us, so we can agree with His Word in confession. Out of the abundance of the heart, the mouth speaks (Luke 6:45). If you continuously entertain evil or negative thoughts in your heart, sooner or later, you will do or say them.

I agreed with Matthew Henry when he said: "It is bad to think ill, but it is worse to speak it, for that implies consent to the evil thought and a willingness to infect others with it." Another writer said, "Wise men think without talking, fools reverse the order."

Learn to say things the right way, in the right place, at the best time, and to the right person. Getting one or two off the list will not help you; you have to get all right. I use the word "learn" because sometimes you have to acquire knowledge before you speak. You might have to pray,

> **If you continuously entertain evil or negative thoughts in your heart, sooner or later, you will do or say them.**

ask questions or seek counsel on how to say what you want to or handle an issue. The wisdom that comes from God can take control of your words so they have value.

A word fitly spoken is like apples of gold in pictures of silver.

(Proverbs 25:11)

We will have to give an account of every idle word we speak on the day of judgement.

Delete the Junk

I went by the field of the lazy man,
And by the vineyard of the man devoid of
understanding; And there it was, all overgrown
with thorns; Its surface was covered with
nettles; Its stone wall was broken down.

(Proverbs 24:30-31)

O NE DAY, I received a notice that I was approaching the storage limit of my email box. So I decided to go through my emails and delete the not so important ones in a bid to create more space for new emails. As I started trying to create space, I discovered the emails taking up the majority of space were not important to me. The essential emails didn't weigh so much, whereas the spam and other unnecessary emails were very big. Immediately, I began to reflect on the situation and to ask myself if unhelpful things were consuming much space and time in my life. I prayed and asked God to uproot every weed and useless things in my life trying to choke my productivity.

No wise farmer would allow his farm to be overtaken by weeds and thorns, instead of legitimate crops. No one plants weeds, but have you noticed their ability to grow anywhere in abundance? Nobody deliberately asks for spam emails but somehow they just come. A farmer can't be blamed when his soil produces weed, but if he does nothing about them, it's a different story. Worse still is if he starts nourishing and giving them more space to flourish. So it is with our hearts and lives. Things may crop up. Things we didn't calculate would happen to us just come from seemingly nowhere. What do we do about them?

How we respond to what happens to us is most important. When thoughts of pride, jealousy or lust come, what do you do? Do you allow them to settle and take up space in your mind or do you delete them? Also, how do you spend your gift of 24 hours? What percentage do prayer and study take up? What about Facebooking, watching movies, work, sleeping, etc.? Let us ensure unnecessary things are not occupying the space of the necessary.

> **No wise farmer would allow his farm to be overtaken by weeds and thorns, instead of legitimate crops.**

Returning the Second Time

Keep on asking, and you will receive what you ask for. Keep on seeking, and you will find. Keep on knocking, and the door will be opened to you.

(Matthew 7:7, NLT)

I GOT UP ONE early morning and started preparing for an appointment I had at the police station. I needed a document from them. On my way, I stopped at a grocery store to get some cash from the cashier since the nearest Automated Teller Machine (ATM) was further down the road and I did not want to be late for the appointment.

Upon entering the store, I decided to organise myself a little bit. So I put down my knapsack on one of the empty counters, took out my credit card from the bag, and then put on my jacket, which was in my hand. I joined the queue and when it was my turn, I asked the cashier if I could withdraw cash from my card. She tried twice, but it wasn't successful; my type of card declined to release cash from the till.

Frustrated and panicky about time, I eventually had to rush to the next ATM down the road. Only one person was there using the machine and no one was in the queue. I went after the lady and in a haste, I pressed the wrong button. I withdrew R1000, instead of the R100 I needed. I shoved it all in my bag, hurried to the police station, went to the front desk and asked to meet the lady with whom I had booked the appointment.

The gentleman said to me, "Sorry, but the lady is not in today."

I said, "But I booked an appointment with her for today."

He responded, "Yeah, but she isn't here today."

Super disappointed, I decided to go home and better prepare for university. Since I had rushed out in the morning, I didn't pack everything I needed for class that day. As I got to the gate of my house, I checked for my keys but could not find them. Oh no! Where could they be? I figured I had lost them. Without my keys, I couldn't do anything.

All my keys were on that bunch: office keys, home keys, gate keys, etc. But I knew I had only made two stops excluding the ATM, and I didn't think a big bunch of keys would fall without notice. So I went straight to the grocery store and asked if anyone had found a bunch of keys. They all said they saw nothing, including the supervisors and coordinators. I then hurried to the ATM and looked around the area. I was panicking. I rushed to the police station, and they said I did not leave any keys there. Where were my keys?

I was puzzled, but I also had a gut feeling I should return to the grocery store because that was where I put my bag down. I spent the most time there, and it was the only place I could have left something without noticing. While these thoughts were going through my mind, I was also wondering why I was having such an unpleasant start to my day. After all, I had said my morning prayers. Now, in retrospect, I know why it happened—so I could write about it.

I went back to the store and saw the manager. It seemed as if she was just staring at me and not saying anything. I felt uncomfortable and discouraged by that. I was just looking around by myself, not knowing what to do next.

Desperate, I walked up to her and said, "Please, are you sure you didn't see any keys because I am almost certain that this should be the place I lost mine?" Once I said that she raised her voice and said, "Oh, I was just hoping you would return and ask again. Just after you left, one of the cashiers handed in your keys. I was hoping you would come back. Here, have your keys."

Startled, I said thank you, not knowing what else to say. I figured she did not even recognise me when I came in. It appears she did not even know I was there until I summoned the courage to ask about the keys the second time.

That was my story that morning. Once I got my keys, the rest of the day was fruitful and beautiful. I found grace and favour with the other day's activities.

If it is yours, even though you did not get it the first time, try again; go again; ask again.

So now I write to you about returning the second time—or maybe a third or fourth as long as God is leading you to something.

If it is yours, even though you did not get it the first time, try again; go again; ask again.

Don't Eat That Stew

Make sure that no one is immoral or godless like Esau, who traded his birthright as the firstborn son for a single meal.

(Hebrews 12:6)

Jacob cooked a stew, and Esau came in from the field weary. Esau said to Jacob, "Please feed me with that same red stew, for I am weary." Therefore, his name was called Edom.

But Jacob said, "Sell me your birthright as of this day."

And Esau said, "Look, I am about to die; so what is this birthright to me?"

Then Jacob said, "Swear to me as of this day."

So he swore to him and sold his birthright to Jacob. And Jacob gave Esau bread and a stew of lentils; then he ate and drank, arose, and went his way. Thus Esau despised his birthright.

(Genesis 25:29-34)

I N THE PRECEDING passage, we read about an incredibly shocking, evil deal. So many things about this deal alarmed me when I read it. What! How could he do that? How could he give up his birthright for a bowl of stew?

One interesting thing about the passage is that Jacob spelt out the cost of the stew. It wasn't hidden from Esau. He said it outright: "Sell me your birthright as of this day." I would have thought on hearing that, Esau would have said: "No way! That's very unfair! I am not buying that for that price. Don't be sneaky!" But instead, he said, "Look, I am about to die; so what is this birthright to me?" Obviously, he must have been very exhausted and probably not thinking straight.

Discipline might be painful for a while but in the long run, it produces the fruit of peace and righteousness. It makes you succeed.

When we are in such a state as Esau, we need the Word of God to save us from the attacks of the Enemy. When you are at your wit's end and feel exhausted, do not make rash decisions. Run to Jesus. Run to the Word. Take up the shield of faith. Resist the devil, and he will flee. Choose to temporarily "suffer," so you can maintain a lasting victory!

Jesus faced a terrible temptation from the devil in the wilderness (Matthew 4:1-11). After fasting 40 days and 40 nights, Jesus was hungry. This probably seemed like a good time for the Enemy to try to make Jesus fall, but thank God for the weapon of the Word. Jesus used the Word of God skilfully and overcame the devil's deception. Jesus did not eat the devil's porridge because He knew He had something much better ahead.

We can also learn from Joseph's reaction when he faced a terrible temptation from Potiphar's wife in Genesis chapter 39. She pressured him day after day to commit fornication with her, but he firmly resisted. When in her lust she grabbed his clothes, he left the clothes in her hands and fled. In his situation, fleeing was the right thing to do. Sometimes we must run away from the environment of the temptation. May God give us wisdom. In Jesus' name.

Coming back to the story of Jacob and Esau, we see the lie the enemy told Esau, which made him justify his actions. Esau said, "Look, I am about to die; so what is this birthright to me?" I think this is still one of the lies the devil makes people believe when he wants to tempt them. He tells them they will die if they don't do certain things, so they forget about the consequences of their actions.

You will not die if you refuse to fornicate. You will not die if you stop stealing. You will not die if you forgive and forget about seeking revenge. You are not about to die!

Discipline might be painful for a while but in the long run, it produces the fruit of peace and righteousness. It makes you succeed.

When people believe "they are about to die" they tend to disregard future consequences as if saying "Let me enjoy the pleasures of today while I live." The problem is if you live only to enjoy the unholy pleasures of today, you will experience many worries tomorrow. Consequent to Esau's bad deal, he worried, laboured, and suffered a lot because he yielded to the temptation of eating that porridge. So please don't eat that unholy stew. It might be red, and it might be hot. But avoid it!

Sharing in the Sufferings of Christ

And after you have suffered a little while, the God of all grace, who has called you to his eternal glory in Christ, will himself restore, confirm, strengthen, and establish you.

(1 Peter 5:10)

S EVERAL SCRIPTURES IN the Bible talk about the sufferings of Christ. Jesus Christ suffered many things on the earth before He ascended to heaven. To suffer means to bear, tolerate, put up with or endure. All the things Jesus suffered were His choice. He willingly accepted them looking forward to the joy ahead.

For as the sufferings of Christ abound in us, so our consolation also abounds in Christ.

(2 Corinthians 1:5)

But rejoice to the extent that you partake of Christ's sufferings, that when His glory is revealed, you may also be glad about exceeding joy.

(1 Peter 4:13)

From the above verse, it is clear there is a reward in partaking in the sufferings of Christ. When we do so, we also partake in His comfort and glory. Another scripture that highlights this truth is in Romans 8:17:

> *And if children, then heirs—heirs of God and joint-heirs with Christ, if indeed we suffer with Him, that we may also be glorified together.*

In what ways did Christ suffer and how can we share in His sufferings? Christ suffered in many ways. While He was on the earth:

- He suffered betrayal (Luke 22:48)
- He suffered rejection (Matthew 27:21-22)
- The King of kings allowed Himself to be scourged, beaten, and spat on (Matthew 26:67-68).
- He was deserted and left alone (Matthew 26:56).
- He was falsely accused because they hated Him.
- He was mocked and ultimately, they crucified the Lord on the cross of Calvary.

How can we share in the sufferings of Christ? If we obey and walk with God, our experiences will give us opportunities to partake in Christ's sufferings.

> *Yes, and all who desire to live godly in Christ Jesus will suffer persecution.*
>
> (2 Timothy 3:12)

If you submit your life to Christ, you might lose some friends, sponsors, relationships with family members, and face rejection.

If you are honest in your dealings, some people will hate you. Why? You are not a fraud. Hence, they cannot rope you into any fraudulent dealings for their benefit. If you are humble enough, some people will spit on you. Maybe not physically, but they might want to take advantage of your so-called "weakness."

If you are spreading the good news, you might experience, rejection, betrayal, and mockery. Ultimately, we have to constantly deny our flesh. We must put its wants and desires to death to experience the true life and glory of Christ. When we suffer with Him in these ways, we can expect to share in His glory, experience the miraculous in this life, and ultimately, reign with Him forever.

> **Ultimately, we have to constantly deny our flesh.**

Sing O Barren

*Sing, O barren, you who have not borne! Break
forth into singing, and cry aloud, you who
have not laboured with child! For more are the
children of the desolate Than the children of the
married woman," says the Lord.*

(Isaiah 54:1)

H ERE IS A very challenging demand. The scriptures say the
barren should sing. This is in contrast to what the world
expects someone in that position to do. Many people think if you
are barren in any area of life, you should mourn. They believe
barrenness should naturally produce mourning or sadness. But
not so with the supernatural. The Bible says, "Sing, O barren."

Do not wait until you become fruitful to start praising God.
If you have not borne, "break forth into singing and cry aloud."
We can learn many lessons from this scripture. We are taught
about God's expectation of us in times of waiting. When our
faith is being tested, when we are waiting on God for a child,

harvest, breakthrough or some other need, He still wants us to praise Him and be thankful in those darkest times.

The Bible gives us examples of people who were courageous enough to sing even in the midst of seemingly hopeless situations. Paul and Silas in prison readily come to mind (Acts 16:25-34). I imagine they looked around at their desperate situation: hands and legs bound, but they recognised their mouths were free.

Their enemies did not realise how powerful their mouths were. If they did, perhaps they would have tried to bind them in some way. In any case, thank God their mouths were free to praise Him. And they did! Those two men bound in chains opened their mouths and belted out praises to God in the dark prison, and their breakthrough came.

Is there an area of your life that seems barren? Why not praise God? That area will not remain barren forever. The wall of Jericho must have been there for years. Hence, it seemed like a foolish idea to attempt to conquer it but even more foolish to do so by singing. Nevertheless, every God-idea is a powerful one. Joshua obeyed and praised God. What happened? The walls came down. I pray that as you sing and praise God through the difficulties in your life. You will become fruitful and possess your land. In Jesus' name.

> Nevertheless, every God-idea is a powerful one. Nevertheless, every God-idea is a powerful one.

Perfecting Me

The Lord will perfect that which concerns me;
Your mercy, O Lord, endures forever; Do not
forsake the works of Your hands.

(Psalm 138:8a)

T HE PRECEDING VERSE is very comforting and personal.
I believe God deals with us as individuals. He knows our strengths and weaknesses. God knows what to let come your way. He knows you can bear it. That is why it is wrong to compare yourself to other people. The Bible says all things work together for good to them that love God and are called according to His purpose (Romans 8:28).

As God is working to perfect all that concerns you (fulfilling His purpose in your life), you might go through very peculiar situations. You might think "But no one else is passing through something like this." You might ask, "Why me?" As

> Not all our experiences look, feel or sound good, but with God on your side, He can turn everything around for His glory and make you smile.

long as you remain focused on God, love Him, and keep His commandments, do not be alarmed. You are uniquely designed, and He knows your frame. That's why your experiences are unique. The good news is that God will perfect all that concerns you. He knows best how to do that. The expectations of the righteous shall not be cut short.

Jesus wants to meet you when He appears in glory, so God is working everything out for your ultimate good. Not all our experiences look, feel or sound good, but with God on your side, He can turn everything around for His glory and make you smile. Let not your heart be troubled. God is working everything out for your good. He is perfecting that which concerns you.

God's Mercy

So then it is not of him who wills, nor of him who runs, but of God who shows mercy.

(Romans 9:16)

A NY WISE CHRISTIAN who has studied the scriptures and observed some patterns in life would be persuaded that God's mercy is very vital for success. One very important prayer a Christian must say daily is, "God have mercy on me." God's mercy makes the difference. It is unquestionable.

God's mercy can launch you into your greatness, as well as silence all your enemies and accusers. God is supreme. There is no higher judge to take your case to. The supreme judge needs to rule in your favour because if God is for us, who can be against us?

Mercy means we don't get what we deserve!

David was not "sinless" in his own right. At least, the Bible records two sins he committed: adultery and murder. But God had promised David sure mercies (Isaiah. 55:3) that extended to his descendants.

Consider Solomon's spectacular offering, that inspired God to give him a blank cheque (1 Kings 3:4-5). I believe it was God's mercy that moved Solomon to make such an offering. We know through scriptures it is God who works in us both to will and to do according to His good pleasure (Philippians 2:13, paraphrased).

Labour and hard work pays off, there is no doubt about it. However, only God can give life to our seeds and sustain them. Every woman who goes into labour prays to deliver a live baby. The beautiful cries or smiles of the baby reassures her the pain and effort were worth it. Much more, as the child starts growing, the pain and thoughts of labour gradually fade.

> God's mercy can launch you into your greatness, as well as silence all your enemies and accusers.

Before you make efforts in any area of life, invite the grace of God to help you. God's mercy crowns it all. Paul puts it this way:

I planted, Apollos watered, but God gave the increase. So then neither he who plants is anything, nor he who waters, but God who gives the increase.

(1 Corinthians 3:6-7)

We know God honours His Word. He told us to ask and we will receive. Therefore, we can ask for God's mercies in prayer. We can also provoke God's mercy by abiding by the Word and principles of God. Even though God's mercies are undeserved, to receive them, it might require our cooperation and submission to God's will.

Consider the life of the Virgin Mary, the mother of Jesus. I am sure there were many other virgins in her generation, but I believe God's mercy and favour singled her out. However, if she was not a virgin, she wouldn't have received that specific favour of giving birth to the Son of God. Why is that? The Bible had earlier recorded in Isaiah 7:14 that *"The virgin shall conceive and bear a son."*

Position yourself to experience the favour of God in your life. To do so, there are some things you must do, protect, and accept. For example, accepting the Lord Jesus Christ as your Lord and Saviour. When you have heard the good news preached to you from time to time but you reject Christ, you will not make it to heaven. No matter how much God loves you, He will not go against His Word. He honours His Word.

Many other people are putting as much effort as you in your generation with respect to righteousness, hard work, discipline, sacrifice, etc. However, the mercies of God can distinguish you. That is why we must ask for God's mercy and grace.

The message is for you to be hardworking, diligent, and pursue God's holiness without which no eyes will see the Lord. Also, be sanctified, dedicated, committed and do not neglect to ask God for His mercy and favour, for by strength shall no man prevail.

It Is the Bees That Produce Honey

Seest thou a man diligent in his business? He shall stand before kings; he shall not stand before mean men.

(Proverbs 22:29)

MANY PEOPLE LIKE honey and constantly talk about all its wonderful benefits. Honey has a wide range of applications. It can be used as a medicine, skin care therapy, an energy booster, for baking, and many other things. But how is the honey made? In simple terms, honey is made by the hardworking bees.

During spring, they suck out nectar from the flowers. The honey stomach hold approximately 70mg of nectar. The bee must visit between 100-1500 flowers to fill up its honey stomach.

One lesson to learn from this is that hard work and diligence may not look attractive or fun in the present, but they are enormously rewarding.

Another interesting thing to note in the honey-making process is that the honey we eat comes from the flower nectar that the honey bees suck up, regurgitate, and dehydrate. This process enhances its nutritional properties and makes the famous substance almost everyone likes.

Take a moment to think about these three major processes: collecting or sucking up, regurgitating, and dehydrating. A lot of people have received many gifts, talents, and special abilities from God but diligence is what transforms the raw gold into something very useful to others.

The bees suck up nectar, which is the raw product, but they break down the complex sugars into easily digestible monosaccharides through the process of ingesting and regurgitating.

It is important to note that it takes hard work to process what God has deposited in our lives, so it can be useful to others.

One lesson to learn from this is that hard work and diligence may not look attractive or fun in the present, but they are enormously rewarding.

The Power of Preparation

[Put first things first.] Prepare your work outside and get it ready for yourself in the field; and afterward build your house and establish a home.
(Proverbs 24:27, AMPC)

WE CANNOT UNDERESTIMATE the power of preparation in all areas of life. As the popular saying goes, "If you fail to plan, you are planning to fail." Failure to prepare limits your chances of success but proper preparation makes room for excellence.

It is wise to deliberately think through any upcoming events. Be positive that all will go well as planned. Prepare in prayer. Consider the logistics and make room for contingencies knowing we live in an imperfect world.

Consider the story of the ten virgins in Matthew 25:1-13. Five of them were wise and the other five were foolish. One significant difference between the two groups was that the wise group thought carefully about their journey and planned appropriately. They didn't just rush out of the house. They prepared and took extra oil with them. Packing the extra oil while preparing might have taken them some additional time, but it was worth it in the long run.

Before you start anything that is important to you, be it your day, a project, marriage, ministry, etc. take some time to prepare for it. Prepare spiritually, physically, emotionally, and otherwise. In practice, this might involve praying and seeking Godly counsel, as well as reading a book on the topic you need information on, so you don't become a victim of ignorance.

Failure to prepare limits your chances of success but proper preparation makes room for excellence.

Preparation may also involve gaining some skills: driving, programming, first aid, etc. that might be a bonus to what you are about to embark on. Do not leave all things to chance because it might not always deliver what you want.

Of course, as Christians, the Holy Spirit should take pre-eminence in our lives and all our plans. This means we should be flexible and willing to interrupt any plan for the Holy Spirit who knows it all.

Sometimes you may find you want to watch a Christian movie but the Holy Spirit is nudging you to pray. Allow Him to take the lead. He always has your best interest at heart. Jesus spoke highly of the need to prepare and plan ahead of a major event when He shared the parable in the book of Luke 14:28:

> *For which of you, intending to build a tower, does not sit down first and count the cost, whether he has enough to finish it.*

By Day and By Night

And he provided light at night with a pillar of fire.
This allowed them to travel by day or by night.

(Exodus 13:21, NLT)

F ROM THE ABOVE scripture and many others in the Bible, we see that God is very conscious about time. He always expects His children to be productive and fruitful. The Bible says God went ahead of the children of Israel in a pillar of cloud by day and a pillar of fire by night to give them light. The cloud and fire guided them in their travels by day and night. Interestingly, God did not want them to waste the night.

Ordinarily, they would have been able to travel by day with the guidance of the pillar of cloud. However, at night they would have to stop because they could not see in the darkness. So the almighty God made a provision for His children, so they could travel by day or night. He made sure they were not limited by the natural changes in time.

God is awesome. He makes sure His people have access to His special grace that can make them fruitful at all times. With

His grace, they cannot be stopped by the weather, economy, sun, moon or anything at all. This promise is clearly stated in Isaiah 60:20,

> *Your sun shall no longer go down, nor shall your moon withdraw itself; For the LORD will be your everlasting light, and the days of your mourning shall be ended.*

Though the Israelites traveled by day and night, it does not mean they did not have the time to rest. When the pillar stopped, the children of Israel rested. When it moved, they followed. In practice, as you walk with the Holy Spirit, you might find He asks you to wake up in the night and pray while others are sleeping. In His time, He gives you rest.

Whenever it seems God is asking us to do something out of the norm, rest assured He will provide the means. Just as He placed the pillar of fire to produce light, He will make provision from His limitless supply, so you can give from your little and accomplish much from what appears to be a limited situation.

Make Some Profit

So he called ten of his servants, delivered to them ten minas, and said to them, 'Do business till I come.'

(Luke 19:13)

RECENTLY, I HAD to do a major sorting of different items in our house because we were relocating. As is the case when people are moving, I started by sorting out the things I had not used for about 6-12 months. I planned to throw them away because, in my opinion, they were not very useful since I hadn't used them for a very long time.

I desperately needed to reduce the amount of luggage we had to carry. When I had finished sorting out those things I had not used for a very long time, I noticed a lot of valuable items among them; most of them were gifts from people. Kind people had given me these costly and precious gifts but unfortunately, I did not use them.

I quickly noticed three categories of these valuable gifts. Some were just not good fits. They were probably given by people not close enough to know my right size or the kind of things I would use.

Category number two had the gifts I had outgrown. And the final category had the ones that were useful and very precious to me, but I just thought the best way to preserve them was not to use them. I just wanted to keep them for good memories.

I want to relate the last category of gifts to the attitudes some Christians exhibit toward the grace and gifts of God. Some people do appreciate the gifts of God in them. They look at themselves and say, "Wow! I thank God for my salvation. See how He has blessed me. He has given me good health, a stable job, beautiful children, and a lovely voice. I can write well. I can evangelise. I can preach well, etc." The sad news is that after acknowledging all these wonderful gifts and blessings, some people do little or nothing with them.

We were saved to play an instrumental role in the salvation of others. Therefore, we need to spend our energy and time doing the work of God and investing in eternity. Our spiritual gifts are not given to us for decoration but to be blessings to the body of Christ.

Unlike physical gifts, the beautiful thing about spiritual gifts is they do not depreciate when used. Rather, they multiply and increase when being utilised to bless others. Let us not only value the grace and gifts of God in our lives. Let us put them to use, for in doing so, God is pleased. I pray in Jesus' name that we will not be like those described in 2 Timothy 3:5 (NLT),

> **Our spiritual gifts are not given to us for decoration but to be blessings to the body of Christ.**

They will act religious, but they will reject the power that could make them godly. Stay away from people like that.

Getting His Permission

Commit everything you do to the LORD. Trust him, and he will help you.

(Psalm 37:5)

O NE AFTERNOON WHEN my 2-year-old son finished his meal, I said to him, "Son, you can go and watch your cartoon now." You should have seen the excitement on his face when I said that. He swiftly sped off, ran to the room with excitement, and continued watching the cartoon.

As I watched him run off, I realised that there were two main reasons why he was super excited when I told him he could go and watch his favourite video. First of all, he liked the cartoon very much but most importantly, I had explicitly given him permission to go and watch it. My permission meant he could come to me if he needed any help getting the video up and running (turning up the sound, magnifying the screen, etc.). He knew if he went off on his own without my permission, he would have a problem asking me for any help with the video. Of course, since I was the one who permitted him to watch the video, I would be more than happy to help him get it set up.

In the same light, we need to seek God's permission in anything we do. This gives us the confidence to approach Him for help over any hurdle we might encounter. If you only follow your ideas or those of your mentors, family, and friends, are you sure they can help you through any storms you might encounter? God has already explicitly asked us to do certain things. His revealed will includes preaching the gospel, helping orphans, widows, and those in need. We should be confident when doing God's will because we know He will back us up. If we encounter any challenges as we go about doing them, we can confidently run to Him for help.

We also have God's specific will. This includes knowing God's mind in relation to particular aspects of our lives: who to marry, which career to pursue, which church to attend, etc. As said earlier, it is important to seek God's will and get His permission, so

> **We should be confident when doing God's will because we know He will back us up.**

we can boldly approach Him in challenging times. I love the scripture in 1 John 5:14-15 (NLV),

> *We are sure that if we ask anything that He wants us to have, He will hear us. If we are sure He hears us when we ask, we can be sure He will give us what we ask for.*

Sowing and Reaping

*Do not be deceived, God is not mocked; for
whatever a man sows, that he will also reap.*

(Galatians 6:7)

M ANY PEOPLE AGREE that the golden rule of sowing and
reaping is true. Several religions accept that we all reap
what we sow. If this is true, and I believe it is, then why do we
still practice evil?

There are several reasons why evil still prevails, even when
the person sowing evil believes he will reap what he has sown
sooner or later. One of the reasons is that without Christ, we lose
control over what we want to do. Sin makes a person its slave
and coerces a man to do what he ordinarily does not want to do.
Then, it leaves you to dance to the music you have been forced to
play. This is an evil under the sun.

Paul, in his letter to the Romans, puts it this way,

*I have discovered this principle of life—that when
I want to do what is right, I inevitably do what*

is wrong. I love God's law with all my heart. But there is another power within me that is at war with my mind. This power makes me a slave to the sin that is still within me. Oh, what a miserable person I am! Who will free me from this life that is dominated by sin and death?5 Thank God! The answer is in Jesus Christ our Lord. So you see how it is: In my mind, I want to obey God's law, but because of my sinful nature I am a slave to sin.

(Romans 7:15-17, NLT)

Thank God! Jesus Christ is indeed the answer. God has given Christians the power over sin through the Spirit of Christ who lives in us. Thus, He has given us the blessing of righteous living, so we can pray "Lead us not into temptation." Every evil habit that was in us before giving our lives to Christ will fade away. We build up our spirit-man by constant studying of the Word of God, praying in the Holy Ghost, as well as fasting and praising God. When we do this, we are empowered to sow good seeds and expect to reap righteousness, peace, and joy in the Holy Ghost.

When I Fell

If you think you are standing strong, be careful not to fall.

(1 Corinthians 10:12, NLT)

I WOKE UP ONE bright day and after saying my prayers, I was eager to get downstairs to kick-start the day's business. Unfortunately, as I placed my feet on the first step on the stairs, I slipped and fell way down to the last step. To my pleasant surprise, I did not hurt myself much, but I did ponder on some facts. First, I was amazed that one tiny slip off from the first step could get me to the very last one.

> **Sin makes a person its slave and coerces a man to do what he ordinarily does not want to do.**

I gradually began to meditate on this experience, I thought about how if we allow seemingly little sins to thrive, they can quickly get us to a place we never imagined. One tiny slip can lead to another. Those little foxes (procrastination, compromise, pride, disobedience etc.) can have negative impact on our lives.

Also, if you go for a hike on the mountain you would realize how easy the journey is to come down the mountain that it is to go up.

Do everything to make sure that you are standing and ascending.

Set a watch on your heart and actions. Engage in things that will move you forward, eliminate loose ends that can make you fall. Love God, love yourself and love people and always remember there is nothing ordinary about you.

> **Do everything to make sure that you are standing and ascending.**

Many blessings!

Glossary

AMPC- The Amplified Bible Classic Edition

ESV- English Standard Version

NIV- New International Version

NLT- New Living Translation

NLV- New Life Version

From the Authors

THANK YOU FOR reading **Nothing Ordinary About You: Inspiring and Motivational Words from a Christian Perspective.** We hope that you were inspired, motivated, and encouraged.

If you would like to let others know about this book, here are some actions you can take to do so.

1. Please visit the site where you purchased it and write a brief review.

2. Tell your friends and family about the book.

3. Consider buying it as a Birthday, Christmas, New Year or Graduation gift for your loved ones.

If you would like to get notifications of new releases and special offers on our books, please join our email list by visiting victorspress.com or sending an email to victoria@victorspress. com.

Remain blessed and remember there is **Nothing Ordinary About You.**

Sincerely,

Victoria & Gibson

Printed in Great Britain
by Amazon